Break on Bethlehem Street

A Christmas Play

Frank Ramirez

CSS Publishing Company, Inc.
Lima, Ohio

BREAKDOWN ON BETHLEHEM STREET

Copyright © 2012 by
CSS Publishing Company, Inc.
Lima, Ohio

For more information about CSS Publishing Company resources, visit our website at www.csspub.com or email us at csr@csspub.com or call (800) 241-4056.

ISBN-13: 978-0-7880-2640-9
ISBN-10: 0-7880-2640-2   PRINTED IN USA

Dedicated to Tom and Betty Lamb

Thanks for your support in ministry, art, and life!

Notes Before Performing

Breakdown on Bethlehem Street was written for a particular church at a particular time. **Make changes!** The cast came from the small town of Everett in Bedford County, Pennsylvania. Sheetz is a well known chain of service stations in the area that include a convenience store and food service. There's a joke about turning to Bedford instead of Everett for help. Our Roman Legionnaire was hard of hearing because he'd ridden in the bubble beneath bombers during World War II. Change the references to this and the name of the convenience store as well as the names of the towns to something that will resonate with your church. The play was performed with script in hand and with costumes.

This play was performed episodically between musical numbers, scripture readings, litanies, and prayers at a worship service. At the most, this play will be twenty minutes long. Combine scenes if you need to. Our church ran scenes 2 and 3 as well as 6 and 7 consecutively. In the case of the latter we had the organist and/or pianist play a stanza from a hymn to separate the change in locale.

Breakdown on Bethlehem Street

Characters
Christi (teenager)
Rachel (teenager)
Eric (teenager)
Mom
Roman Legionnaire
Joseph
Mary
Angel
Baby Jesus

Props
Cell phone for each teenager
Manger
Baby Jesus (live or doll)

Scene 1

(a living room; two sisters and a brother are together)

Christi: I guess it *is* Christmas.

Rachel: Almost.

Eric: Doesn't seem the same.

Rachel: Well, it's a recession.

Christi: You said the "R" word. I'm gonna tell Mom.

Eric: Go ahead. But I warn you, I don't think she has much of a sense of humor.

Rachel: Yeah, right. You know, everyone says it's a recession, but we still have cell phones and high-speed internet.

Eric: Maybe, but we don't call out for pizza as often. And we eat a lot of leftovers.

Christi: Leftovers are good.

Eric: The first time or two. Also there's not as much money around.

Christi: *No* money.

Rachel: Yeah, but thanks to FaceBook and Twitter we know it faster than ever.

(enter Mom)

Mom: Hi kids. What ya doin'?

Christi: Not much. Thinking of going out for a soda.

Mom: Will you be back for the Christmas Eve service?

Rachel: Yeah.

Christi: Sure.

Eric: Probably.

Mom: "Probably" better be a word for "yes." I don't feel like going alone.

Rachel: If we're late, go without us. We'll catch up.

Mom: No, you be on time. It starts at 7:00.

Eric: Mom, it gets crowded at the Sheetz. We might be late.

Mom: Don't let me down. You know what Christmas does to me. I get so blue.

Christi: But it's Christmas. What is there to be blue about?

Mom: I just am. It's not going to be a great Christmas, you know. There's a recession going on.

Rachel: I thought we weren't supposed to use the "R" word.

Mom: Well… didn't want to let you down.

Eric: Mom, you're a great Mom. You didn't let us down.

Mom: It's not you guys. It's life. It's — I don't know. Why do they even have Christmas? My mother died around Christmas. The plant closed last Christmas. Bad stuff happens around Christmas.

Christi: I know. Can we get you something?

Mom: You know what I'd like? You know what I'd like some Christmas?

Rachel: Tell us.

Mom: Just once, just once, I'd like to hear an angel.

Christi: Would you settle for a Diet Pepsi?

Mom: Sure, and if they're out, get me a Diet Coke. Or a diet angel. I don't care. Now listen, I meant what I said. Don't be late.

Eric: We won't.

(exit all)

———————

Suggested reading:
Luke 2:1-3
"Let all mortal flesh keep silence" (v. 1).

Scene 2

(enter Eric, Rachel, and Christi, looking very puzzled)

Eric: Okay, I admit it. We're lost.

Rachel: How can anyone get lost in Everett?

Eric: Don't blame me. I wasn't the one navigating.

Christi: What's to navigate? We were going to Sheetz.

Eric: You yelled shotgun! Shotgun is navigator. That's the rule.

Christi: And backseat is ventilator. That's the fool.

Rachel: What does that mean?

Christi: It means I'm just a little scared. Where are we?

Eric: We're somewhere. We didn't get far down the road. Just some fog on Main Street.

Rachel: Yeah, I was afraid to drive in the fog. I couldn't see anything. So I pulled over and stopped and then the car wouldn't start again.

Eric: You mean you couldn't start the car. I could've started the car.

Rachel: You don't have a license.

Eric: Minor point.

Christi: I don't even see buildings. This is Everett? Where are the buildings? This is creepy.

Rachel: You know, it's kind of creeping me out too.

Eric: *(points out to congregation)* Hey, people are coming. Stay close to me.

Christi: Why? You afraid?

Eric: No. I just want to keep *you* all safe.

Rachel: Who are all these people? They don't look like anyone from Everett!

Christi: We must have taken a real wrong turn. What is going on?

Rachel: They all look like they're dressed for 2,000 years ago. I get it! It's a casting call. Someone's making a film.

Eric: Ooh, I want to be an extra. Let's find out who's in charge.

Christi: I don't think so. Mom said she wanted us back on time.

Rachel: Mom also said she wanted to hear an angel. I don't think that's going to happen either.

Eric: Let's find out who's the boss around here. Hey! Hey you!

Christi: Guys. I've got a great idea. Let's find out who's cast as the angel in this picture to bring back to church. Abracadabra — we'll make Mom's wish come true.

(enter Roman Legionnaire)

Legionnaire: Well, hi there. How are you three? You look lost. *(shakes hands all around)* Can I help you?

Rachel: Yeah, like who's in charge? Can we talk to the director?

Legionnaire: In charge? The emperor's in charge.

Christi: Emperor? What emperor?

Legionnaire: The emperor of the Roman Empire. Who else? You look lost, you three. Are you sure you don't need help?

Christi: Where are we?

Legionnaire: You're right outside Bethlehem. We're about five miles from Jerusalem.

Eric: What's going on here?

Rachel: Sister, brother, I don't think we're in Kansas anymore — or Everett either.

———————

Suggested reading:
Luke 2:4-6

Suggested musical interlude:
"O Little Town of Bethlehem"

Scene 3

(Eric, Legionnaire, Rachel, and Christi stand together)

Eric: Who are all these people?

Legionnaire: They're folks like you, from all over. They've come here for the census.

Rachel: Census?

Legionnaire: Caesar says that everyone is to go to their hometown to be registered for the taxes. I'm here to keep order.

Eric: And who — what are you?

Legionnaire: I'm Sonnyus Dickensius. I'm a Roman legionnaire. Can't you tell from my flat feet? *(laughs)*

Christi: We are lost. We are *really* lost.

Legionnaire: Maybe I can help. Where are you from?

Eric: Everett, in Pennsylvania.

Legionnaire: Never heard of it, and let me tell you, that's saying something. I've been everywhere. I've served in the Roman army all over the empire. Some people don't like serving here in Judea, but let me tell you, I've been in much more dangerous places.

Rachel: Really? Where?

Legionnaire: Back when I was in Asia Minor they slung me underneath an elephant, almost like I was in a bubble. That was a pretty dangerous place to be when all the armies were charging at each other. That's why my hearing's no good. Them elephants are loud.

(exit Legionnaire; enter Mary and Joseph. Mary is very footsore and tired. She is leaning on Joseph.)

Joseph: Just a little farther, Miryam. I'm sure we'll find a place to stay soon.

Mary: I hope so, Yosef. I've been walking for three days and I'll bet this baby is coming.

Joseph: No, it's too early.

Mary: The baby doesn't think so.

Rachel: Oh no. I don't believe it. I just do *not* believe it.

———————————

Choir Number, Solo, or Duet

Scene 4

(Joseph and Mary stand together and Rachel, Christi, and Eric are nearby.)

Rachel: Guys, what's going on here?

Christi: We're lost.

Rachel: Oh, we're not lost. We've found something — or something has found us.

Eric: What are you talking about?

Rachel: Unless I'm totally crazy, that's Joseph and Mary and this is 2,000 years ago and the baby Jesus is about to be born.

Christi: You're right. You're totally crazy.

Eric: *(goes to Joseph)* What's your name?

Joseph: Yosef.

Mary: And I'm Miryam, and I'm about to give birth.

Eric: And what are you going to name your baby?

Joseph: We're going to name him Yeshua.

Eric: *(to Rachel and Christi)* What a relief. For a crazy Moment I thought we'd gone back in time 2,000 years and come across Joseph and Mary about to give birth to Jesus. But this is just Yosef and Miryam and they're going to call their baby Yeshua. *(to Mary and Joseph)* Hey, hope things work out. Best of luck. Come on, guys. Let's go.

Christi: *(to Mary and Joseph)* Where's your donkey?

Mary: Donkey?

Rachel: Donkey? What are you talking about?

Christi: Don't you guys ever pay attention during the sermons? Yosef? Miryam? Yeshua? That's Aramaic for —

Rachel: Don't say it!

Christi: Joseph. Mary. Jesus.

Mary: *(cries aloud)* Oh no! I think it's getting to be time. We've got to do something. We've got to get somewhere.

Joseph: *(to Christi)* What's this about a donkey?

Christi: You're Mary. You're Joseph. You have a donkey. You ride a donkey. You're eight months pregnant. What are you doing walking from Nazareth to Bethlehem when you're eight months pregnant?

Mary: *(cries aloud again, then speaks)* We don't have a donkey. We're poor people from Nazareth. We walk everywhere.

Rachel: You're walking and you're eight months pregnant?

Joseph: What are we supposed to do? Sprout wings and fly like angels?

Mary: Don't make Yosef feel any worse than he already does. We're so poor. And this baby, this poor baby. Why me? Why me?

Joseph: *(tries to comfort her)* I think it's because you said "yes." *We* said "yes," and I had that dream.

Mary: *(enter Angel, who stands to the side; no one sees her right away)* That was then. There was an angel in the room then. This is now. There's no angel here. There are no angels anywhere. Where's an angel when you need one? I am so tired.

Joseph: Hold on, Miryam. We'll get help.

Mary: I hope so. I don't want to have this baby out in the street. Why can't anyone make room for us? Where are we going to go?

Eric: This is *not* the way it looks in the Christmas cards.

Joseph: What are Christmas cards?

Christi: You send them out every Christmas and they've got you and Mary and the baby on them — with snow. And it always looks peaceful.

Rachel: *(gets a little panicky)* And there's a donkey. There's always a donkey. *(Mary cries aloud again)*

Eric: We have to do something!

Rachel: What? I don't know nothing about birthing no babies.

Christi: Stay here. We'll get help.

Mary: What kind of help?

Rachel: I don't know — help.

Joseph: I'll go with you.

Eric: No you won't, Yosef. Don't leave her alone. We'll be right back.

Christi: *(suddenly notices Angel; the Angel is just a little edgy, kind of with an attitude)* What are *you* laughing at?

Angel: You guys.

Rachel: Who are you?

Angel: Not who. What. Come on. You've been talking about Christmas cards. Don't you recognize me?

Eric: Should I?

Angel: *(spreads out her arms)* I'm an angel.

Rachel: We're saved!

Angel: What do you mean, "we"?

Time of Offering

Scene 5

Angel: *(spreads out her arms)* I'm an angel.

Rachel: We're saved!

Angel: What do you mean, "we"?

Eric: Where are your wings?

Angel: I'm not that kind of angel. Wings are for the angels who escort the stars in their dance across the heavens. Angels that are a little too full of themselves, if you ask me. Anyway, you guys had better get started if you're to save this situation. It's starting to look a little serious. *(Mary cries out)* Make that *very* serious. So what are you guys going to do?

Eric: Why us?

Angel: Why not you?

Rachel: Why not *you?*

Angel: It's not my job to save this situation.

Christi: Then whose is it?

Angel: Yours.

Eric: How? Our cell phones don't work. There aren't any towers here. Have you noticed? Our car doesn't work. There's no internet connection. What do we have?

Angel: You have a heart. And you have a chance.

Rachel: Why us? We're nobody special. Why is this happening to us? We're just some kids from Everett.

Angel: So I should get some kids from Bedford?

Rachel: No, I'm just saying.

Angel: And I'm just saying that you're looking at just some kids from Nazareth. For them Bethlehem is like going to Pittsburgh.

Eric: Pittsburgh? Really?

Angel: Okay, maybe Greensburg. So, are you going to save this situation? It's starting to get dark. It's just going to get harder to find help. *(Rachel walks off)* Look, you don't have to do something big. You just have to do *something*. Sometimes something is just enough.

Eric: All right, but you've got to do something for us.

Angel: What?

Eric: Our mom wants to hear an angel. So if we help here, you have to come back. Okay?

Angel: Deal.

Rachel: *(re-enters)* Hey guys. There's a cave. Right over here. I can see some straw at the entrance. Maybe they use it for animals.

Christi: What good is a cave? Jesus was born in a barn.

Rachel: Yeah, but what kind of a barn? Don't you remember those pictures the pastor showed when he got back from the Holy Land? There was a picture of a cave and they said that was the place Jesus was born.

Eric: Did you go inside? Is it safe?

Rachel: No way! I don't have a light. I'm not walking into a cave when it's dark.

Eric: You have a phone.

Rachel: Great, I'll call the exterminators and have them go over it. Are you kidding? There are no towers here.

Eric: The phone's got a light. Unless your battery's dead.

Rachel: Oh, right. *(thrusts her phone at Eric)* You look inside. There might be bugs.

Eric: *(exits)* I'll be right back.

Christi: Hey, Yosef — Miryam — we might have a place for you.

Joseph: *(helps Mary to her feet)* Good. Miryam can't last much longer. *(Rachel helps hold Mary up)*

Eric: *(re-enters)* I don't believe it. The cave is used for a barn. There is straw everywhere on the ground, and there are some animals and a kind of a wooden thing that has hay in it.

Rachel: A kind of a wooden thing that some people call a manger?

Eric: Maybe.

Mary: Hurry! I'm about to have a baby.

Joseph: Hurry. She's about to have a —

Eric: I know. I know.

(together they all walk off)

––––––––––––––––

Suggested reading:
Luke 2:7

Instrumental, perhaps piano solo:
"What Child Is This?"

Scene 6

(Mary is seated, holding a baby — a live baby if possible. Joseph is kneeling beside her. Angel is standing over them. Rachel and Christi are fanning Eric, trying to get him to wake up.)

Joseph: Is your friend going to be okay?

Rachel: He just fainted. It's what guys do.

Christi: Let me get a picture of this. *(She points cell phone at Eric. She then turns and points it at Joseph and Mary.)* Let me a get a picture of you guys too.

Mary: A what?

Christi: Never mind.

Eric: Where am I? What happened?

Mary: A baby happened. Thank you all so much for helping us find this place.

Joseph: We were so tired we couldn't think straight. It all just caught up with us. *(pauses)* I'm sure you don't know, but there's something very special about this baby.

Eric: Oh, we know; trust us, we know.

Christi: I can't believe it. We're here. We're here at the birth.

Angel: Actually, everyone's at the birth of — you know. Whether it's playing at the nativity set, playing Christmas music, listening to kids sing, or looking at a Christmas card.

Joseph: There you go talking about Christmas cards again. What are they?

Angel: Don't worry about it. Ah, but how about you guys? Aren't you supposed to be somewhere?

Rachel: Oh no! Mom's expecting us to be at the service. We're late.

Christi: Er, aren't we about 2,000 years early for the service? And we've got a good excuse.

Eric: And a car that doesn't work.

Angel: Try turning it around and pushing it back into the fog. I think you'll be surprised.

Eric: Hey! Don't forget — you're coming along with us.

Angel: If I must, I must. *(to Mary and Joseph)* I think you two will do fine. And if you're hungry, don't worry. There are some shepherds on the way. They can get you guys something to eat.

Mary: How do you know some shepherds are on the way?

Angel: Trust me on this one. Guys?

(Angel exits with Rachel, Christi, and Eric)

Suggested reading:
Luke 2:9-12
(angel's words)

Suggested hymn:
"The Virgin Mary Had a Baby Boy"

Scene 7

(Mom is seated, watching whoever is making music. Angel, Rachel, Christi, and Eric enter and step behind her.)

Eric: Mom! Mom!

Rachel: Sorry we're late.

Mom: *(rises to hug them)* I am so glad to see you.

Christi: Sorry, we had car troubles. I know you only asked us for one thing, to go with you to church…

Mom: It's all right. I figured you were having fun at Sheetz. I just walked over. At first I was a little hurt, a little angry, but then, you know that one thing I wanted…

Eric: Two things, really. Didn't you want a Diet Pepsi?

Rachel: Don't bring it up, all right? Mom, the car's all right!

Mom: *(smiles)* Actually, the only thing I really wanted was to hear an angel.

Eric: Guess what? We took care of that! *(pushes Angel forward)*

Mom: Who's your friend? Nice to meet you. Can you come over for dessert after worship?

Angel: Sure, that'd be fun.

Eric: Mom, that one thing you wanted —

Mom: So you took care of it? You took care of all this music? Because it's been like listening to an angel. *(Mom lists what she has heard that evening)* And we haven't even gotten to "Silent Night." You know, I'd been feeling really blue about things, but I'd forgotten. Christmas is the little things we do for each other. Christmas is the fellowship we share in Jesus Christ. Can I tell you kids something?

Christi: What is it?

Mom: I feel like I've been to the manger. Like Christmas has happened for me the first time all over again. I don't know why I was so blue. Okay, I *do* know why I was so blue. But it doesn't seem to matter somehow. You know, walking here tonight the stars were so bright I felt like I could reach out and touch them. And the little clouds were just like angels flying across the heavens. And listening here tonight — nothing but angels. *(Angel slips away)* Listen, I'm sorry. You kids must think I'm silly. But I've decided that it's the angel in your heart that matters the most. Quiet. *(looks toward congregation)* They're getting ready for "Silent Night."

Rachel: What really happened tonight? Were we dreaming?

Christi: Then we were dreaming the same dream.

Eric: Rachel, look at your phone. *(Rachel looks at her phone)*

Rachel: Ah… it's a little smudgy, but that's definitely Miryam and Yosef. And the little baby. *(she pushes a button)* And that's definitely Eric after he fainted.

Eric: Hey! Erase that!

Rachel: Are you kidding? I'm not erasing anything.

Christi: So Mom saw her angel. Hey, where did our angel go?

Rachel: Right here — right here in our hearts.

Eric: I hope we don't all get heartburn.

Mom: No, it won't be heartburn. I think we're all getting a case of heart*warm*. And I hope we never recover.

———————

Suggested reading:
Luke 2:19

Suggested hymn:
"Silent Night"
(perhaps by candlelight)

The End

CPSIA information can be obtained
at www.ICGtesting.com
Printed in the USA
BVHW04s0819011018
528935BV00015B/149/P

9 780788 026409